# JOHN WA

*A Life from Beginning to End*

Copyright © 2019 by Hourly History.

**All rights reserved.**

# Table of Contents

# Introduction

Shakespeare once asked, "What's in a name?" And when you think about the name of John Wayne, it is a very famous name indeed. The funny thing is, John Wayne was not born with this moniker at all—it was actually one that had been fixed onto his person later in life. He came into this world not as John Wayne, but as Marion Robert Morrison. Later, his name changed to Marion Mitchell Morrison because his parents decided to name their next son Robert. To eliminate confusion, however, we will from henceforward primarily refer to this famous movie legend as the larger world knows him, by the name of John Wayne.

Wayne graced the screen as a cowboy, an all-around rugged hero of the plains. With his "pull yourself up by your bootstraps" determination and raw sense of individualism, in many ways he came to symbolize everything that Americans held dear. His characters, tough as nails, were always idealistic adventurers seeking to right the wrongs of the world. In this book, we will cut through all the hype and get to the real man behind the legend of John Wayne.

# Chapter One

# The Boy Named Marion Morrison

*"Tomorrow hopes we have learned something from yesterday."*

—John Wayne

John Wayne was born as Marion Robert Morrison on May 26, 1907, in the town of Winterset, Iowa, to Clyde Morrison and Mary "Molly" Morrison. His mother and father were merely 20 and 19 years old when they got married. The couple did not wait for the official blessings of their parents or the church; instead, they were wed by the Justice of the Peace on September 29, 1905. At first, Molly was thrilled with her new husband and thought that she had made a good catch. Clyde was handsome, educated, and had prospects lined up to get a job as a pharmacist in Waterloo, Iowa. He seemed like a good pick, someone that would take care of her and set her mind at ease.

Unfortunately, Molly would be mistaken, because although Clyde could be a hard worker (when he did work), he was also just as hard of a drinker. It was this lethal combination that would threaten to send the family into ruin. As a result, as soon as Wayne was old enough to work he did so in order to help provide for his family and their ever-increasing bills. At the tender age of ten, he was leaving early in the morning to deliver papers, just to bring home extra cash to put food on the table. Things began to look up, however, when Wayne's father received gainful employment in 1916 as a pharmacist in Glendale, California.

The home that Wayne's family lived in was a small but comfortable house situated right in the middle of downtown. It was maybe a little rough around the edges, but it was home. Rather than a playground or a baseball diamond, the two main places that John Wayne spent time at was a sawmill and the local lumberyard. Wayne also had some rather interesting neighbors. He apparently lived right next door to a gun runner for the famous Mexican revolutionary Pancho Villa. According to Wayne's later recollection, the neighboring family's fortunes would fluctuate depending on how well the gun trade was going. When the gun trade was doing well, they had a lot of money, and when business was scarce they would be "eating beans."

After the move, little John Wayne was signed up to attend the fourth grade at nearby Sixth Street Elementary School. Besides work and school, the family also began to attend the local Methodist church. Wayne, eager to escape the dysfunction of his parents, when he wasn't working found time to join the Boy Scouts and logged hours at the local YMCA. By 1919, at the age of 12, Wayne was in the prestigious Troop Four level of the scouts, and although he never attained the rank of Eagle Scout, he would stay an active member all the way up to his High School graduation.

Wayne became a student at Union High School. Here he managed to make some pretty good grades as well as excel in school athletics—especially football, a sport which he would use to produce the physique for which he was later famous. He was also quite active in the drama department of his school, an activity that turned out to be the training wheels of his future career.

One eccentricity that Wayne became known for early on was the fact that he would always walk to school accompanied by his huge Airedale Terrier named Duke. The locals got a kick out of this and began calling Wayne "Little Duke" as a result. The name stuck, and he would carry it for the rest of his life. Even after he had developed the stage name of John Wayne, he always told those who knew him best, "Just call me Duke."

# Chapter Two

# College Football and Family Troubles

*"Talk low, talk slow, and don't say too much."*

—John Wayne

In many ways for John Wayne, childhood came to an end when his parents divorced and went their separate ways. In this breakup, not only did Wayne's parents go their separate ways, but he and his brother Robert would part company as well, with Bobby opting to stay with his mother while Wayne would continue living with his dad in Glendale. Wayne knew that his family had reached a point of no return, and sadly, family life and childhood would never be the same again.

In the midst of the turmoil, Wayne tried his best to stay busy. His days usually consisted of getting up in the early morning to deliver papers, then spending the day in school, and helping out at his father's pharmacy after that. During his teenage years he also often helped out at a local horseshoe manufacturer. Believe it or not, it was this gig making horseshoes that ended up being Wayne's first connection to Hollywood since the horses that his employer shod shoes for were used in productions based out of Hollywood studios.

Immediately after John Wayne graduated from High School in 1925, he put in an application for the United States Naval Academy hoping to try his luck in naval command, but after filling out the paperwork, his application was ultimately rejected. As fate would have it, Wayne ended up going to the University of Southern California instead. Due to his football prowess he was offered a full-ride scholarship, covering all of his tuition and even meals in the student cafeteria, which meant a lot back in the 1920s when academic funding was typically much more scarce and hard to come by.

It is said that in considering a major, Wayne figured that studying law would be the most prudent course to take, since real estate was so big in California, and there was always need of someone to interpret the legal dealings of property. In college, Wayne also pursued his avid interest of football, playing on the University of Southern California football team. By this time, Wayne is said to have reached his full 6-foot 4 height and weighed around 170 pounds.

According to many of his female acquaintances at the time, Wayne was also said to have been "drop dead gorgeous." With dark brown, curly hair, blue eyes, and delicate cheekbones, he was said to really stand out from a crowd. In fact, according to a former classmate, "his looks alone could stop traffic." But apparently as good looking as the young John Wayne was, he was a bit awkward around the opposite sex. It is said that he was quite shy, and it took quite a while for him to warm up to someone. He is said to have been very well liked, but his dates at that point were actually few and far between. Wayne's main outlet in college was always football—at least until a fateful injury would stop his athletic career.

# Chapter Three

# On the Set with Ford

*"The man was my heart. There was a communion between us that not many men have. I have never been closer to any person in my life."*

—John Wayne on John Ford

The next major milestone in Wayne's life was in the spring of 1926 when Wayne's coach Howard Jones managed to get him and a couple of other guys on the team a summer job on a set for Fox Studios. Jones was a friend of Tom Mix, who just so happened to be a director. As Jones explained to his players, "I got Tom Mix a good box for the football games. He said if there was ever anything, he could do for me, he would do it." And he was right, as a favor for Jones, Mix did indeed hire some of his players—including Wayne—to work as extra stagehands for the summer. According to Wayne, they got the job after going to the studio and presenting a letter of recommendation from Jones. They were then introduced to Mix who happily informed them, "a star owes it to his public to keep in fine physical condition. I want you to be my trainers."

Shortly after this statement, the players were put on the official payroll for the production of the latest western that Mix and his crew were shooting. As Wayne recalls, they were introduced to Mix on Friday and then reported to work the following Monday. Yet according to Wayne, the short weekend in between was still enough time for the busy movie mogul to forget all about him. Wayne would later recall that once they were on the lot, they encountered Mix driving up in his car. Wayne greeted Mix with, "Good morning, Mr. Mix," but all he received was a blank look in return. Nevertheless, the group was indeed on the payroll whether the guy who hired them remembered them or not. For the rest of the summer, Wayne would make $35 a week lugging heavy props and other furnishings across the stage, from set to set. This was a great boon for Wayne who was able to pay off the debt that he had been accumulating.

After this production, Wayne's next big break came to pass in September of 1926, in the form of a film called *Mother Machree*. In this film, Wayne had the distinction of herding a wild flock of geese. As bizarre as it sounds, this was the odd job that he held down—herding geese that were used in certain scenes back into their pens when they were not needed. Wayne didn't take such a mediocre role very seriously, and he would often joke with other members of the crew about his lowly position on the set. Wayne was doing as much one day when he suddenly heard someone shout, "Hey goose herder!" It was the director, a blowhard kind of boss by the name of John Ford.

Ford, who himself used to be a ball player back in college, had apparently heard that Wayne was hired on under the recommendation of USC's football coach. This had sparked his interest, prompting him to inquire, "You're one of Howard Jones' bright boys?" At which Wayne responded, "Yes." Ford, an aggressive and naturally combative kind of character, then shot back with the challenge, "And you call yourself a football player?" Wayne is said to have blithely responded with something like, "I guess so," as Ford continued, "You're a guard, eh? Let's see you get down in position." Upon hearing this, as if on cue, Wayne then dropped down into a classic three-point stance.

Ford then mercilessly kicked Wayne's hand out from under him, causing Wayne to fall down flat on his stomach. As Wayne struggled to get up, Ford then mocked him, "And you call yourself a guard. I'll bet you couldn't even take me out." At which Wayne defiantly mumbled, "I'd like to try." Without another word, Ford accepted this challenge and after marching off several feet spun around and charged at John Wayne. But instead of simply tackling Ford, Wayne chose to place a foot out and trip the director, causing him to dive headlong to the ground. Ford sat there stunned for a moment. A dangerous silence filled the set, as everyone stared and watched to see what the director would do. Suddenly, Ford burst into raucous laughter. Hearing their boss laugh, the crew then loosened up and began to laugh as well. The friendship Wayne forged with Ford that day would last a lifetime.

# Chapter Four

# Becoming John Wayne

*"I'm not the sort to back away from a fight. I don't believe*
*in shrinking from anything. It's not my speed; I'm a guy*
*who meets adversities head on."*

—John Wayne

In one of those classic turning points in life, Wayne would be delivered a severe setback during his days at USC in the form of a shoulder injury. The accounts of exactly what happened vary. But according to those who say they were there, the incident occurred at a California beach where Wayne attempted to body surf. Wayne was apparently trying to impress some girls with his moves when he hit some rough waters and ended up getting thrown by the waves back onto the beach where his shoulder was violently dislocated and his collarbone broken.

Rendering him unable to play football any longer, Wayne's injury would not only sideline him from the game, but it would also sideline him from the university since it took away his only means to pay for his tuition—his scholarship. There was no way around it; if he couldn't get his scholarship renewed, Wayne would have to find another way to pay. This meant taking on odd jobs on studio sets and—if he could manage it—signing on for small walk-on roles in films.

Times were hard for Wayne, and he was getting threadbare. But although his financial situation was turning rather grim, his personal life would soon perk up in a big way when a blind date arranged by a friend would turn into nothing short of a date with destiny. John Wayne was still a little shy in college, and his friends thought that a blind date might help get him socially motivated. The date was with a local girl named Carmen Saenz, in which the pair arrived along with a few other couples at the Rendezvous Ballroom located in the vicinity of California's Newport Beach.

The date went fairly well, and afterward Carmen invited Wayne over to her house. Carmen still lived with her parents at the time, so this was by all means an innocent extension of their date. It was here at Carmen's family home, however, that Wayne found himself caught in what could only be called love at first sight. The object of his love wasn't Carmen—it was her sister Josephine. As soon as Wayne laid eyes on her, he knew he wanted to be with her, and apparently with Carmen's blessing, they began to go out together on a regular basis.

But as much as Wayne and Josephine enjoyed each other's company, her parents were none too thrilled. First of all, they didn't care for the age gap the couple presented, since Wayne was a 19-year-old university student and Josephine was a 16-year-old high schooler. Even if they could get past the age difference, they couldn't quite get past Wayne's background. The Saenz family was fairly well to do, and they knew that Wayne came from a disadvantaged family which was unable to pay his own way in college.

Today, such concerns would be absurd. But back in the 1920s, in affluent circles, being able to put your kids through college was a sign of wealth and prestige. The few poorer students that managed to get their tuition paid with a scholarship, such as the one John Wayne had, were derisively referred to as "scholarship boys." Josephine's father, José Saenz, wasn't about to have his daughter get into a serious relationship with a scholarship boy. Truth be told, even Wayne's grip on his scholarship was tenuous at best. Without his scholarship, he was on his own, and unable to pay he was ultimately forced to drop out.

Wayne was now really not sure what to do with himself, but as fate would have it, his old football coach provided him some unforeseen direction. Back to the drawing board once again, Wayne would then spend the summer of 1927 working as a prop handler. He decided to take a year off school so that he could save money for the rest of his tuition and hopefully return to USC in the fall of 1928. The first job that Wayne was able to get with Fox was another Ford production entitled *Four Sons*.

His main role was as the guy who dumped leaves onto a fan just off screen so that they would float down onto the set, in full mimicry of fall weather. Although innocuous in nature, this scene was very important for the production team and had to be done several times in order to get it just right. This put John Wayne in the tedious position of continuously dumping leaves, sweeping them up, and then dumping them again. Wayne was growing weary of the retakes, and somewhere along the way lost his order of operations and found himself sweeping up leaves when he should have been dumping them, completely messing up the shot. The crew was frustrated, but when Wayne realized what he had done, he was even more aggravated and threw his broom down, marching right off the set in what amounted to an exasperated tantrum.

Even though Wayne had just walked off the job, Ford was apparently once again entertained by what he perceived to be John Wayne's sense of comic relief in action. Wayne was then brought back to Ford where Wayne actually bent over as Ford proceeded to give him a "kick in the ass." Wayne had clearly endeared himself with John Ford, but it wouldn't be long before he would get on the temperamental director's bad side as well.

The next Ford production that Wayne was a part of was called *Hangman's House*—a 1928 film that was an epic depiction of legal troubles, discord, and angst. The role that Wayne was placed in was small but somewhat memorable. He was a fiery young Irish youth who worked up a fury and stomped down a section of a picket fence. This troubled character was then eventually brought before a hanging judge who mouthed the words, "You shall hang by the neck until you are dead, dead, dead." The actors merely mouthed their lines since this was a silent film with subtitles. But upon being exposed to such an odd line, Wayne couldn't help but laugh, and instead of following the script he let out a comical, "Amen!" This bit of adlibbing did not sit well with the director, Ford, at all, and he immediately began shouting for Wayne's removal, screaming, "Get that son of a bitch out of the prisoner's box! Get him off the stage! Get him off the damned lot! I don't ever want to see him again!" But this time, the bark was much worse than the bite, and after a couple of days, John Wayne was brought right back onto the set.

Wishing to check out some of the other studios, Wayne next sought a job with Warner Brothers, getting a stint in a production of *Noah's Ark*, where he got paid $15 an hour as an extra. He was then able to get a significant upgrade, being cast in 1929's *Salute*, increasing his pay to $75 a week. In this film, Wayne played a Navy officer by the name of Bill who subjected his crew members to constant hazing. Wayne then got his next big break by chance when the director Raoul Walsh observed Wayne lugging furniture in one of his prop jobs and thought that the ruggedly handsome young man would be the perfect pick for his new leading role.

Walsh wanted to make a big-time western based upon a popular *Saturday Evening Post* serial called "The Shaggy Legion." This was the beginnings of an epic production that Walsh would ultimately call *The Big Trail*. Walsh was looking for a young cowboy pioneer to ride the plains, and he thought that he saw that in John Wayne. He approached Wayne and struck up a conversation, "What else can you do besides handle props?" At which Wayne responded, "I can play football." Raoul then agreed, "I believe you."

Shortly after this exchange, Wayne was taken for his screen test. At first, it didn't go so well with Wayne later recalling that the effort was just a bit too Shakespearean for him. But they tried again shortly thereafter, and Wayne was finally able to find his groove. The screen test consisted of someone asking him various basic questions pertaining to the script, such as, "How long was the trip? Will we see buffalo?" Instead of answering them, however, Wayne shot back his own improvised questions in a defiant style that would become characteristic of his film persona. He cagily asked, "Why do you want to go west? Can you handle a rifle?"

Apparently, Raoul Walsh was very pleased with Wayne's delivery, and feeling he found his star yelled, "Cut!" Wayne was hired. It was shortly after this that the head of the studio, Winfield Sheehan, came up with the idea of giving John Wayne, who up until this point had been known as Marion Morrison, a new name. It is said that Sheehan and Walsh had come up with the idea of naming Morrison after a general from the Revolutionary War called "Mad" Anthony Wayne. But after some discussion, it was decided that Anthony was just a bit too Italian, so the first name of John was settled upon instead. Wayne himself was not even present for the discussion.

At any rate, this is how John Wayne came to be. The Little Duke from Glendale had come a long way and was—in every sense of the word—making a name for himself.

## Chapter Five

# The Big Trail and the Big Disappointment

*"When you come to see a picture of mine, I want you to know that I'm not going to do anything that will make you uncomfortable. I want you to know that you won't be disappointed with me."*

—John Wayne

*The Big Trail*, living up to its name, was a big production, and as such the studio purchased and built multiple props and used several miles of land in the creation of the film. The production team also partnered with a cattle rustler by the name of Jack Padjan, using him as a talent scout for Native Americans at a nearby reservation in Wyoming. Here Padjan gathered several members of the Arapaho tribe who were interested in making their debut as extras in the movie.

It was while John Wayne was lost in the shuffle of production for this feature film that his parents' long-time separation was finally, officially settled as a formal divorce on February 20, 1930. Wayne's father Clyde would later go on to marry a 29-year-old divorcee, who was not too much older than John Wayne himself. Such facts didn't bother Wayne much; in the end, he just wanted his dear old father to be happy.

During the spring, Wayne began to work on the production in earnest, starting with publicity shots of him standing with guns drawn. The official shooting of the film then began on April 20, 1930, and wouldn't finish until August 20. During this window of time, Wayne was dedicated and determined, waking up every single day around five in the morning and working well into the night. Under this heavy workload, Wayne was struck with a severe bout of diarrhea—not exactly the stuff of star power—but apparently it was so bad that Wayne had to call off work for a couple of days just to recover. He didn't want to stay gone long, however, because he knew that he could be very easily replaced.

Struggling to get back on set, Wayne had lost about 18 pounds at this point. He was exhausted, but through sheer force of will, he got himself back behind the camera. The first scene he shot was certainly not very considerate of his condition, as he was made to film a scene in which he and a few other cowboys guzzled down hard liquor. The combination of whiskey and the previous sickness took their toll, and immediately after shooting, Wayne would recall that he quite literally, "puked and crapped" blood for several days thereafter.

There was a lot of other intrigue going on the set of *The Big Trail* as well. For one, there has long been a rumor that Wayne was having a fling with leading lady Marguerite Churchill. In addition to this drama, there was also frequent fights on and off the set among extras and stagehands. Robert Parrish, who was a young extra at the time, would recall that the grandson of Geronimo, Charlie Stevens, would get into it with a rugged stagehand by the name of Cheyenne Flynn. Geronimo's grandson had apparently been accused of cheating at cards, and Flynn wasn't going to take such things lying down. It is said that Flynn leaped upon Stevens, and in a moment of pure primal aggression that predated Mike Tyson's famous ear biting by several decades, he screamed, "I'm going to bite your ear off!" The next thing anyone knew Stevens let out a horrible scream. Flynn let him go, and Stevens took off running in the other direction.

The witness to this altercation, Parrish, would then claim that the very next day he stumbled upon what appeared to be a "piece of Steven's ear covered with ants." The story sounds rather far-fetched, but there can be no doubt that the world of Hollywood was much rougher in the early twentieth century than it is today. And there were indeed regular fights among participants. Just as they were wrapping up filming of *The Big Trail*, Wayne would be pulled into one of these tussles himself.

Wayne had been sitting in his train car, making a trip back to the Hollywood set, playing a game of cards, when he was alerted to a horrible altercation ensuing a few train cars down from him. A stagehand had come back to inform him that some stuntmen were mercilessly pummeling Frederick Burton, a fellow actor from the film. In being given this bit of information, Wayne, viewed as a cool-headed peacemaker, had apparently been automatically volunteered to break up the fight. As it turns out, the man was being attacked at the behest of none other than the direction of film, Raoul Walsh. Walsh believed that the man had been fooling around with his wife, so he sicked his stuntmen onto the actor to "teach him a lesson." Wayne was the one who learned a lesson, however: he learned that he didn't care much for Raoul Walsh, and on that day lost any admiration or esteem that he may have had for him.

Nevertheless, despite all of the drama, *The Big Trail* finished production and made its debut at Grauman's Chinese Theatre in October of 1930. The movie was not exactly a big hit, but it was a major production, clocking in at just over $2 million. For his work on the film, John Wayne made about $105 a week, which was decent money back in those days. But since the film did so dismally, in the end it proved a big letdown for John Wayne. As a result of the lackluster reception, Wayne would not get offered another leading role until about a decade later. He had set his fortunes with *The Big Trail*, and it had turned into one of the biggest disappointments of his life.

# Chapter Six

# Stuck in the B-List

*"I suppose my best attribute—if you want to call it that—is sincerity. I can sell sincerity because that's the way I am."*

—John Wayne

After *The Big Trail* turned into the big disappointment, Wayne was now once again struggling to find work, and for his next role, he only managed to get a small part in the production of *Girls Demand Excitement* which he began work on in November of 1930. Shortly after production of this piece came to a conclusion, Wayne received a six-month contract with Columbia for a movie called *Men Are Like That*, which was actually an adaptation of the play *Arizona*. Although the name may sound like a typical cowboy film, it isn't. In this feature, Wayne is cast in the role of a football player who falls in love with several women before abandoning them. A typical film drama that only received moderate success but in retrospect is believed to have captured much of Wayne's early style.

Wayne's next move was to sign on with Mascot in late 1931, where he agreed to do several serial features. One of which was a piece called *The Shadow of the Eagle* which was shot during December of 1931. Wayne worked hard during the production process of all these projects and was once again engaged in a breakneck schedule of arriving on set early in the morning and not leaving until late at night.

Following *The Shadow of the Eagle*, Wayne then got to work on another Mascot serial, this time a version of *The Three Musketeers* which was filmed between April of 1932 and April of 1933. It was later that summer, on June 24, 1933, in the midst of this heavy workload, that John Wayne married his long-time girlfriend Josephine. A priest married the pair in traditional Catholic fashion at the Church of the Immaculate Conception. Soon after this union, the couple would have a steady line of children, starting with the birth of their son Michael in 1934, their daughter Antonia in 1936, their son Patrick in 1939, and another daughter they named Melinda in 1940.

In between the creation of all of these descendants, John Wayne continued his habitual mediocre roles in mediocre films. Even though Wayne was getting paid well for his work, the longer he was stuck in this rut of lackluster productions, his star was growing dimmer and dimmer by the day. Wayne knew that he was at serious risk of being permanently typecast as a B movie hack. He was tremendously depressed about this condition, but there wasn't much he could do about it, staying the course was the only means he had to make a living.

In the middle of all of this professional frustration, Wayne would also have a tragic turn of events in his personal life with the news of the death of his father. His passing was sudden. Clyde had just dropped his step daughter off at school when he mentioned that he wasn't feeling well. After saying bye to his step daughter, he then apparently laid down in bed and died of a massive heart attack. Wayne was beside himself with grief—he had always greatly loved and respected his father despite his flaws.

But nevertheless, as he had done his whole life, Wayne quickly learned to compartmentalize his emotions. The extent to which he had done so would be demonstrated several years after his father's passing. While attending a burial for one of his fellow associates in the film industry, he suddenly looked around the graveyard and offhandedly remarked, "My dad is buried up here someplace. I've never been back since the funeral."

His frustration with his professional situation meanwhile was becoming palpable, and shortly after the passing of his father in 1937, he vented his frustration on his old friend and director Ford, asking him, "When is it my turn?" Wayne recalls that Ford calmly responded, "Just wait. I'll let you know when I get the right script." It was shortly thereafter that Ford would introduce Wayne to the right script—a simple little piece called *Stagecoach* which would forever change John Wayne's life.

## Chapter Seven

# Riding the Stagecoach to Success

*"Nobody should come to the movies unless he believes in heroes."*

—John Wayne

*Stagecoach* was produced by Walter Wanger in the fall of 1938, and Wayne began working on set for the film on October 31. It was Halloween, but when it came to his career prospects, Wayne wasn't hoping for any tricks this time around, and fortunately for him he was in for a real treat. *Stagecoach* wrapped up filming in December of 1938 and was released in February of 1939.

The film had actually been adapted from a play written by Eugene O'Neill. The original story shadows the lives of a group of steamship sailors. John Wayne's character is a freewheeling young man who falls in love with an actress. In the film, Wayne strayed away from the do-gooder type roles that he had previously played and instead stared as a slightly villainous tough guy. It seemed that the new approach did wonders for Wayne, because upon completion, *Variety Magazine* had the following review ready and waiting for him: "John Wayne, as the outlaw, displays talent hitherto only partially used—a forthright, restrained delivery and an appealing personality which here gets a new impetus." Wayne had finally hit the sweet spot of his acting modality—he had now reached mainstream star status, and there was no turning back.

After *Stagecoach*, John Wayne was cast for a role in the film *Seven Sinners* in 1940. In this film, he starred opposite of Marlene Dietrich, and the two soon developed an intimate relationship both on and off the set. Wayne later relayed the story of their first encounter as being a rapid descent into unbridled passion, and it was Marlene Dietrich that had played the major role in bringing them to such a juncture. Marlene, who invited Wayne to her dressing room, allegedly made the first move. As the story goes, Wayne was awkwardly standing around, hovering over Marlene's shoulder as she put on makeup. He tried some small talk but was so nervous that all he could come up with was an awkward, "What time is it?" To which Marlene cut right through Wayne's anxiety by pulling up her dress and showing him a leg with a watch strategically placed in a garter, bluntly informing him, "It's very early darling. We have plenty of time."

In the movie, Dietrich played a woman intent on seducing Wayne's character, and in real life she appears to have done very much the same. Theirs was a brief romance, however, and they would break it off shortly after it had begun. Unlike many other leading men, Wayne truly did love his wife despite his indiscretions and was usually wracked with guilt whenever he did partake in forbidden Hollywood fruit.

But when his wife eventually found out about some of the goings-on behind the scenes of some of Wayne's films, she was heartbroken all the same. She, of course, did not want her husband to be around such women anymore. Wayne couldn't avoid these starlets, and despite any protestations on his wife's part, he and Marlene Dietrich would remain friends and star in a few more movies together afterward. Most notably they both played a role in the movies *Pittsburgh* and *The Spoilers*, both films produced in 1942.

When she had finally had enough of Wayne's extramarital misadventures, Josephine sought intervention in the form of a priest named Father McCoy who she brought to the Wayne home for marriage counseling. Wayne didn't appreciate the interference, but for the sake of his wife assented to the intervention. The end result had Wayne promising to stop being personally involved with Dietrich, as long as Josie stopped talking about the whole ordeal. He hoped that she would forget about the whole thing and move on, but he was mistaken. Eventually the rift would become so insurmountable that Josephine felt that she had no choice but to file for divorce. John Wayne had apparently ridden the stagecoach to success but had left his marriage vows somewhere back at the station.

# Chapter Eight

# War and Love Affairs

*"All I'm for is the liberty of the individual."*

—John Wayne

After the Dietrich affair, the Wayne marriage was already on the rocks, but it hit absolute rock bottom when Wayne began seeing his new paramour, a lively Mexican woman named Esperanza Baur. Wayne was introduced to Bauer through Dietrich's business manager, a man who went by the name of Bo Roos. In August of 1941, Wayne had accompanied Roos along with a troop of other actors, including fellow star Ray Milland, to Mexico on the premise of finding investors for a new movie studio.

But Wayne found more than he had bargained for when while hanging out at their hotel Milland brought him to the acquaintance of Esperanza Baur, a woman he referred to as "Chata." Almost immediately, Wayne was completely enamored with Chata, and soon she was all that he talked about. He told Roos on one occasion that "the great thing about Latin women was that they liked the simple things—marriage, family, children, a home." Chata was not exactly a simple woman, however, she had been seeing Milland, and she was known to be linked to several other people as well. On top of that, her mother was said to be an actual madam, who ran a brothel in Mexico. Still, Wayne was bitten by the love bug and could not be convinced otherwise. He continued to see Chata regularly even after returning to the United States.

The last straw for Josephine came when she began to receive nightly calls from Wayne's latest mistress asking about his whereabouts. Josie may have been able to look past some of Wayne's indiscretions when they occurred far afield, but now his latest lover was actively infiltrating her private life. This was more than she could take. As a result, shortly thereafter Wayne came home to find all of his clothing piled up on the front lawn, a clear indication that Josephine was done dealing with his extra liaisons. The couple would then file for a separation on June 20, 1942, which would ultimately lead to divorce a few years later in 1945. Shortly after the divorce was finalized, Chata and Wayne were married on January 17, 1946.

While the initial stages of his divorce were underway, the year 1942 also saw John Wayne make his debut on the radio, in which he stared in several serial radio dramas. As the country became more and more involved in World War II, the main bread and butter for all Hollywood stars soon became aimed at the war effort. Wayne was actually able to escape the draft because he had four children to support. His film studio also advocated for him to be excused from the draft "in support of national interest." Additionally, Wayne was in his early 30s at the time and considered past the usual age for the draft.

But even though John Wayne was exempt from the draft, he was not exempt from doing SSO tours for the troops. In all, Wayne would tour countless bases and hospital units in the Pacific theater over the course of three months from 1943 to 1944. He also toyed with the idea of volunteering like some other Hollywood leading men had done, but in the end, he kept finding excuses not to. This fact would come to haunt him for the rest of his life. Many would later claim that Wayne's often great—some would say even exaggerated—show of patriotism stemmed from his guilt over the fact that he failed to serve his nation during the war.

As John Wayne continued to reprise his roles both in film and in real life, he would recast himself as a producer by the end of the decade, directing such films as *Angel and the Badman* in 1947. Playing the lead role in the production, Wayne took on the persona of a conflicted gun slinger who was torn between his wild life and the beautiful Quaker girl that he had become infatuated with. Playing the role of this girl was acclaimed actress Gail Russell. She seemed excellent for the part, and her and Wayne's screen chemistry was almost immediate. This smooth interaction, however, soon made Chata fear that Wayne was cheating on her with his new onscreen love interest. Chata, who had brazenly engaged in an affair with Wayne under the nose of his first wife, was now fearing that she was getting a taste of her own medicine from someone else. Her fear and resentment reached a boiling point on the night of the wrap party for *Angel and the Badman*. When Wayne arrived home late, drunk, he was greeted by Chata who pointed a gun at him and nearly shot him.

Shortly after filming for *Angel and the Badman* drew to a close, reviews of the film began to pour in. Contrary to many of his previous works, this piece was actually well received by most of the critics who viewed his performance in the film as employing a much more complex and dynamic approach. His personal fanbase, however, was not quite so thrilled. This film tended to focus more on the protagonist's romantic entanglements rather than gun battles. This served to alienate much of his audience. Many of the die-hard action enthusiasts were a bit disappointed from this deviation from what had been the standard, shoot-'em-up John Wayne formula.

But John Wayne learned long ago in the movie business that you can't always please everyone. He knew that now that he had found his direction, the best thing for him to do was to keep moving forward. So that was exactly what he did.

# Chapter Nine

# Sands of Iwo Jima

*"Get off your butt and join the marines!"*

—John Wayne

The next major milestone in Wayne's life came with the release of the film *Red River* in 1948. The piece had actually been rather quickly put together on the heels of *Angel and the Badman* and had already been all but wrapped up by the Christmas season of 1946. Here Wayne played a conflicted cattleman named Tom Dunson. It was a darker sort of character, and to Wayne's pleasant surprise, he seemed to play it well. He was a natural in displaying the character's breakdowns and especially his strained relationship with his son, a role that was performed by Montgomery Clift. Wayne was at first skeptical that Clift, who was in his 20s at the time and straight off of Broadway, would be a good fit to play his antagonist in the film. But Clift, an extremely studious actor, soon proved his weight in gold when it came to complementing Wayne's style and persona.

The only problem Clift seemed to have was with drinking, but this was common ground he shared with Wayne, who was already a habitual alcoholic both on and off the set. Nevertheless, some $2 million in production costs later, the movie proved to be a major blockbuster hit. *Red River* is still considered one of John Wayne's best films to this day. But as was often the case in John Wayne's life, this professional positive coincided with a personal negative.

Right after finishing up *Red River*, Wayne had taken his new wife Chata on what they viewed as a belated honeymoon. The couple went off to Honolulu along with Wayne's friend and frequent screenwriter, James Edward Grant, and his wife. Chata didn't approve of the company and claimed that Grant was a bad influence on Wayne who encouraged him to be promiscuous with other women on the set. This viewpoint of Chata's only festered and became worse as she proceeded to drink her way through the occasion. Soon she was becoming unhinged, shouting obscenities at Wayne and embarrassing him in public. It is said that Wayne came back from the trip completely distraught but still reluctant to admit that his marriage to Chata was ill-advised. Chata seemed to have a hold on Wayne and was able to manipulate him into doing whatever she wanted.

The only escape Wayne could find from his ever-increasing marital troubles was by burying his head in his work. Some of his concerned friends might even say he was burying his head in the sand by doing so and merely delaying the inevitable. But speaking of sand, at least this volatile period with Chata was artistically productive for Wayne since it was during this period of turmoil that he starred in the iconic war film *Sands of Iwo Jima*. This film was originally inspired by the famous wartime photo of

U.S. troops struggling to raise the American flag over the war-torn Pacific island of Iwo Jima. Just 750 miles from mainland Japan, this island was to be a stepping stone for an American invasion of the Japanese Empire that had bombed the naval base of Pearl Harbor a few years prior.

Ultimately, the Japanese were brought into submission not by a mainland invasion launched from Iwo Jima, but through the dropping of two atomic bombs. The immense struggle and loss of life (around 7,000 U.S. Marines and 18,000 Japanese troops were killed) that occurred in taking this island was one of the most dramatic episodes of World War II. The folks at Hollywood rightly guessed that the events of Iwo Jima had all of the makings of a blockbuster film if only they could write a captivating script and cast the roles with competent actors. To their credit, the producers of this piece did indeed do their homework, partnering directly with the Marine Corps for onscreen advisors, as well as the use of a whole unit of actual troops to serve as extras on the set. As for John Wayne, with his ever-growing image as the all-American patriot, he seemed perfect for the role he was given.

Cast as the character of Sergeant John Stryker, Wayne played the part of a no-nonsense career soldier who was often disliked by his troops for his harsh demeanor. As he leads his men to battle, however, they come to a new understanding of their commander and grow to respect his dedicated leadership. *Sands of Iwo Jima* was shot over the summer of 1949, from July to August, and released to the public before the year was out. It was an instant success and did well enough to gain Wayne a nomination for Best Actor at the Oscars. Wayne wouldn't take home the coveted prize, however, until 20 years later for his role in the smash hit *True Grit*. But with *Sands of Iwo Jima*, he was well on his way all the same.

# Chapter Ten

# Wayne's Final Marriage

*"We had a pretty good time together, when she wasn't trying to kill me!"*

—John Wayne on Esperanza "Chata" Baur

Despite their previous marital troubles, Wayne and his second wife Chata endured most of 1949 together without incident. But throughout much of 1950, the relationship became strained once again. Before the year was out Chata was demanding that she be allowed to make a trip to Mexico City to visit her mother over the Christmas holiday. Even though it would take her away from her husband during the Christmas season, Chata claimed the visit was needed to cure her of her "nervous condition."

This holiday trip turned into an extended stay, with Wayne's wife not returning to him until the summer of 1951. If this time away from Wayne helped her nerves remains unclear, but Wayne's nerves certainly were not at his best; during this time, he was beset by a personal crisis of a whole other order as his hair began to thin and fall out. Wayne, who always prided himself in his appearance, was at first hesitant to do so, but ultimately decided to start wearing a toupee.

Wayne was in transition in his life, perhaps even hitting what many would refer to as a midlife crisis, when he left Chata behind in their Encino home in 1952 to go to Peru under the pretense of planning a new movie in the Peruvian environs. It was on a local film site in Peru that Wayne would meet the woman that would become his third wife, a young Peruvian woman named Pilar Pallete. Pilar was actually in a similar condition as Wayne—she was married but separated with her long-estranged husband and on the verge of divorce. She later recalled that at the time of the fateful meeting with John Wayne she had not even seen her husband for many months. Her estranged husband was deeply involved with another woman at the time.

After meeting this new love interest, Wayne wasn't wasting any time in moving forward, and shortly after returning to the states, on September 12, 1952, he filed for divorce. Chata appeared more than ready for this official split and quickly contacted all the gossip columns in order to run John Wayne's name in the mud as much as she possibly could. As the divorce proceedings came to a close in October of 1953, Chata would portray John Wayne as a habitual drunk and an abusive husband. Wayne denied any such accusations, and in the end, he was able to get a settlement that was fairly favorable to his estate. Chata meanwhile managed to receive a lump sum of $150,000 and a limited six-year alimony payment of $50,000 per year.

Chata always felt that she received the short end of the stick after the divorce, and sadly her life afterward would not be a very happy one. Following the divorce, she holed herself up in a hotel in Mexico City where she proceeded to drink herself to death. As if her own life was the result of a tragic Hollywood plot twist, Chata was found dead in her hotel room surrounded by empty bottles of booze as her only companions. She was not even 40 years old.

If Wayne mourned the death of his second wife, he was not quite so forthcoming with his emotions. On November 1, 1954, Wayne officially married for the third time, to his new wife, Pilar Pallete. Wed in the luxurious surroundings of Kona, Hawaii, John Wayne was most certainly hoping that the third time would be the charm.

## Chapter Eleven

# Late Life and Lung Cancer

*"Courage is being scared to death—and saddling up anyway."*

—John Wayne

Right around the time of his marriage to Pilar, John Wayne had been commissioned to play the role of Genghis Khan in the film *The Conqueror*. Produced by the reclusive Howard Hughes, the film was meant to be an epic blockbuster but turned out more to be an epic bust. First of all was the glaring fact of just how miscast Wayne was in the role of the Mongolian warlord. In his fake Fu Manchu mustache, bad makeup, and cheesy time period clothing, he stood out like a sore thumb. Secondly, the dialogue was considered completely lacking to anyone who heard it, with Wayne grunting in his fake accent phrases that were barely even coherent. In one scene, he proclaimed to his co-star Susan Hayward, "Know this, woman: I take you for wife."

By today's standards, such a bizarre film wouldn't have got off the drawing boards. Even back in the 1950s, it didn't take much to realize that the production was a complete flop. It was so bad, in fact, that *The Conqueror* would come to haunt Wayne for the rest of his life. Some would argue that filming on-site in the Escalante Desert of Utah, in the fake mustaches, wigs, and makeup of a Mongolian warlord, not only damaged Wayne's credibility but also may have damaged his health. As it turns out, the set wasn't far from where the infamous nuclear bomb tests in Nevada were being carried out. Several years later, it would come to the cast and crew's attention that the desert sand where they shot the film was most likely full of radioactive dust. Wayne himself would have to wonder if the lung cancer he would later develop was contributed to by inhaling this radioactive dirt. Then again, it was no secret that Wayne smoked several packs of cigarettes a day, which in itself was enough to cause lung cancer without any aid from radioactive fallout.

By 1955, Wayne was seeking to recoup from the losses that he experienced from *The Conqueror* in what seemed to be yet another promising western, *The Searchers*. This movie had Wayne back in familiar territory as a gunslinging cowboy. *The Searchers* lived up to every bit of Wayne's cowboy image, and it was the first film that had him utter the phrase that would be his trademark, calling other characters "pilgrim." The film also had an all-star cast consisting of a young Natalie Wood, Jeffrey Hunter, Vera Miles, and Ward Bond.

The plot is built around the character of Debbie played by Natalie Wood and her uncle Ethan Edwards played by John Wayne. Debbie has been kidnaped by a roving band of Comanches, and her uncle is part of a party of searchers attempting to find her. In the end, they do indeed rescue the woman, but she has already been forcefully wed to a Comanche warrior, provoking all kinds of painful drama among the main group of characters. The film is more than just an action adventure—it showcases a dynamic and complex narrative. Along with these big emotions and plot devices, it was also quite an expensive enterprise with a budget that clocked in at almost $4 million. But even at this high cost, it would eventually provide a great return for all of those that invested in it.

Production of *The Searchers* came to a close on August 16, 1955. Shortly after Wayne wrapped up his work on the set, he and his wife Pilar welcomed their first child into the world. Born on March 31, 1956, the happy mother and father named the new baby Aissa. This child—the first of three that he and Pilar would have—came when Wayne was just a few weeks shy of turning 49 years old.

Wayne would continue attempting to balance his film and family life until he hit an unexpected roadblock in 1964 when he was given his lung cancer diagnosis. The cancer at this point was already at such a late stage that he had to have four ribs and his entire left lung removed. After his experience, Wayne, contrary to what his handlers had advised, was inspired to go on a public awareness campaign about his illness, in which he stressed the importance of early cancer screenings. Interestingly enough, it is from these efforts of public awareness that has John Wayne being cited as the originator of using the phrase the "Big C" as a nickname for cancer.

Five years after his original diagnosis, Wayne would be declared cancer-free in 1969. It was that same year, after displaying so much tenacity and courage in his personal life, that he embarked upon one of the greatest films of his professional career, a piece entitled *True Grit*. Another epic western taking place in the latter half of the nineteenth century, *True Grit* casts Wayne in the role of Rooster Cogburn, an intrepid U.S. Marshal. In the film, Rooster Cogburn, a man described as having "true grit," is dispatched to capture a dangerous fugitive and murderer named Tom Chaney. The film debuted at Radio City Music Hall on July 3, 1969, and was a stunning success. It had John Wayne back at what he did best—playing the rugged onscreen hero.

For his efforts, Wayne would ultimately win both the Golden Globe and the academy award for Best Actor. The film was so popular that a sequel would be made in 1975 titled after the main character, *Rooster Cogburn*. Thanks to this success, Wayne would remain a household name for many years to come.

# Conclusion

Despite his success in the box office, the 1970s would be a decade of slow decline for John Wayne. He and his wife Pilar had begun to drift apart, a fact that was ultimately realized in their official separation in 1973. Left to his own devices, Wayne continued to bury himself in his work. He lived his last few years in quiet isolation, with his personal secretary—and sometimes lover—Pat as his main source of company.

Wayne would finally succumb to the dreaded "Big C" as he referred to it, on June 11, 1979, after it made its return as an aggressive form of stomach cancer. After stubbornly resisting the Catholic religion of his past three wives, it is said that on his death bed Wayne was finally won over to the Roman Catholic faith. After his funeral service, John Wayne was put to rest at Pacific View Memorial Park Cemetery in California. He lived an exceptional life. Like so many of the characters he played, John Wayne simply rode off into the sunset while the rest of the world looked on.

Printed in Great Britain
by Amazon